Cambridge English Readers

Level 3

Series editor: Philip Prowse

How I Met Myself

David A. Hill

CAMBRIDGE
UNIVERSITY PRESS

CAMBRIDGE
UNIVERSITY PRESS

University Printing House, Cambridge CB2 8BS, United Kingdom

Cambridge University Press is part of the University of Cambridge.

It furthers the University's mission by disseminating knowledge in the pursuit of
education, learning and research at the highest international levels of excellence.

www.cambridge.org
Information on this title: www.cambridge.org/9780521750189

First published 2001
Reprinted 2015

Printed in the United Kingdom by Hobbs the Printers Ltd

A catalogue record for this publication is available from the British Library

ISBN 978-0-521-75018-9 Paperback

Contents

Characters

John Taylor: an English computer programmer working for a multinational company in Budapest, Hungary.

Andrea Taylor: John's wife, and a teacher of Hungarian.

Kati Taylor: John and Andrea's baby daughter.

Zsolt: a man who has a bar in Budapest's Thirteenth District.

János Szabó: John Taylor's doppelgänger, a Hungarian man who died in the 1956 revolution.

Mrs Fischer: an old lady who knew János Szabó.

Paul Harris: an old friend of John Taylor's.

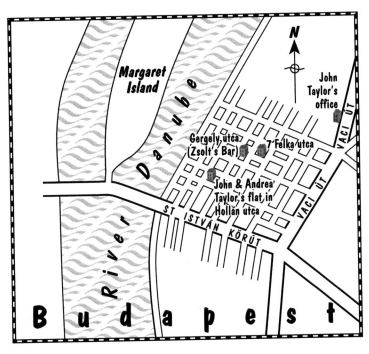

Chapter 1 *A strange meeting*

I was walking home from my office one January evening. It was a Monday. The weather was very cold, and there were some low clouds around the tops of the buildings. Once I'd left the main road, there weren't many people in the dark, narrow streets of Budapest's Thirteenth District. Everything was very quiet. It felt as if the city was waiting for something.

As I walked I thought about what had happened at work. I had argued with one of the Hungarians I worked with. It was the first serious problem since I'd arrived. I was trying to think what to do about it, and I was also hoping that my wife, Andrea, had made one of her nice hot soups for dinner.

After about five minutes it started to snow heavily, so that the streets were soon completely white. As I was walking along a very dark part of one street there was the noise of a door shutting loudly inside a building. Then I heard the sound of someone running.

Suddenly, the street door opened and a man came out of it and ran straight into me. I fell over into the snow, shouting something like, 'Hey, watch where you're going!' – my words were loud in the empty street. The man turned to look at me for a moment. 'Sorry,' he said very quietly, in Hungarian, before walking quickly away.

What I saw at that moment, in that dark winter street was very strange, and I felt very afraid. Because what I saw was *me*. *My* face looking down at me. *My* mouth saying sorry.

Chapter 2   *Getting to know me*

Perhaps I'd better tell you something about me before I go on with the rest of this story.

My name is John Taylor, and I'm 34 years old. I'm nearly two metres tall, with light brown hair and eyes and I have a moustache. I'm a computer programmer. Four years ago, my company in Bristol became part of a very large multinational computer company – you would know the name if I told you. I was offered the chance to go and work in their Budapest office. They needed someone to lead a young Hungarian team in an important new piece of work. I was very pleased. It was a better job in the company, and I thought it would be really interesting to work in another country, one I'd never visited.

Like many British people, I thought I knew three things about Hungary: the Danube cuts the capital into two halves, Buda and Pest; the Hungarian football team had once beaten England 6 – 3 in London, and people eat hot goulash all the time.

There was a lot to learn! And I learnt quickly.

The company sent me to Hungarian language classes at a special school. Hungarian is very different from English. I had one-to-one lessons with a pretty teacher called Andrea. She was a lovely young woman, with dark brown hair, blue eyes and a beautiful smile, and she seemed to understand me very well. Our lessons soon became lessons outside class hours, and slowly we fell in love. Eighteen months later we got married.

Each day of the week I walk to work and back from our flat in the Thirteenth District. I work in a new office on Váci utca, and it takes me about thirty minutes to get there. My usual working day is half past eight in the morning to six in the evening. I generally enjoy my work. The offices are light and modern, and I like the people I work with.

Andrea works at different times during the day, teaching Hungarian to foreigners in a number of schools and companies. She also teaches some students at home.

We live on the Pest side of the city, not far from the Danube. The old part of the Thirteenth District where we live is an area of narrow streets full of small shops, bars and restaurants. It still feels like an old city. And it was in one of these streets that I met myself.

Chapter 3 *A search*

Now I'll continue my story.

I lay there in the snow for a few moments, trying to understand what had just happened. My first thought was, 'Where has the man gone?' I looked along the street, and was just in time to see him turning right at the next corner.

I got up immediately, brushed the snow off my clothes and ran after him. He crossed the road and went into another street. When I got to the corner I saw him going into a doorway. I walked quickly along the empty street, and found it was the entrance to a wine cellar. It was under a block of flats, and you had to go down some steps to get in. It was one of those Budapest places where working men meet to drink, talk and smoke. I looked down the steps. There was the low noise of conversation and a smell of wine and cigarettes coming up to meet me.

I stood in the snow for a moment, deciding what to do and looking around me. I had a strange feeling about going down into the wine cellar. I wasn't sure who I'd find there. I looked at my footprints – the dark marks my feet had made in the new snow. *My* footprints . . . But only *my* footprints! Where were *his*? I looked back along the street. There were only my footprints. My mind was running round and round in circles trying to understand what was happening. I stepped down into the wine cellar. It was the first time I had been into that kind of bar.

Inside, it was suddenly warm after the winter streets. It was dark, and my eyes took a few moments to get used to the darkness. I looked around me – there were a few men dressed in working clothes, standing in small groups, drinking their wine and talking. I looked over to the bar where I expected to see my man buying a drink. But there was just a young man with fair hair talking to the barman. The place was not very big, and I walked around and looked at everyone carefully.

My man was nowhere to be seen. I walked over to the bar.

'Where did the man go?' I asked the barman.

'What man?' he asked back.

'Just before I came in,' I said, 'there was another man who came in. Where is he?'

The barman looked at the blond man with a look on his face that seemed to say, 'Who's this mad man?' I realised that I sounded strange.

'I'm sorry,' I started again. 'I'm looking for a friend – I thought he had just come here. That's why I came in. Are you sure nobody came in just before me?'

'See for yourself,' said the barman, showing me the men in the room.

'But is there no other room here?' I asked.

'Only the toilet,' said the barman, looking at the corner.

I went over and opened the door. It was cold and dirty. And empty.

I didn't know what to do. I decided to stay and see what happened.

'A glass of dry red wine, please,' I said to the barman when I got back to the bar.

He gave it to me. I paid, and then I moved over to an empty place.

There were no chairs, so I stood up against a high narrow table. A television was on in the corner of the room. I watched the news and waited. Andrea didn't know where I was. Nobody came in or went out. I drank another glass of wine. After an hour, I left. I didn't understand anything, and it was not just because I had drunk too much wine on an empty stomach.

*   *   *

'You smell of wine and smoke!' said Andrea, as I was standing by the front door, taking off my coat and boots. 'What have you been doing?'

'Oh, I just went for a drink with Péter,' I said. 'We argued at work today, and I wanted to talk about it because there is an important meeting tomorrow.'

Don't think badly of me – I usually tell my wife the truth! It was just that as I walked home, I had decided it would be better not to say anything about what had happened. When I thought about it, it all sounded so stupid. Someone ran out of a building and knocked me down into the snow. When he turned back to say sorry, I saw that he looked just like me. And then when I followed him he left no footprints. And he wasn't in the wine cellar I saw him go into. It really was all too stupid. So I told her the story about Péter and kept the truth – if it was the truth – to myself.

By now, I wasn't sure if I really had seen someone who looked the same as me! But when I went into the bathroom to wash before dinner, and I looked at my face in the mirror, I knew that I was right. It wasn't just someone who looked a bit like me, it was *me* that I'd seen.

That night, in bed, I couldn't sleep. I kept thinking about what had happened over and over again. Andrea knew something was not right. She moved across the bed and put her arm around me.

'What is it, love?' she asked quietly.

'Oh, nothing,' I replied. 'Just those problems at work again. Don't worry.'

And I kissed her.

Until I met myself, I had always thought myself to be a normal, intelligent person. I thought I understood more or less how the world around me worked, even my new world in Budapest. But what happened that night in the street had changed something inside me, and I couldn't get it out of my mind. I kept seeing myself on the ground in that dark, snowy street, looking up at myself. I felt terribly afraid.

Chapter 4   *7 Felka utca*

As I walked to work the next day – Tuesday – I planned my evening. I had decided that last night the man had come out of the building at about five to seven. I had just been in time to see the start of the seven o'clock news on television in the wine bar, and only a few minutes had passed between him knocking me over and the news. I wanted to go back there that evening at the same time.

The day seemed to take a long time to pass. At work, I had the meeting with Péter to talk about the difficulty of the day before. We talked about our problems and came to a friendly agreement. I had lunch in the office restaurant as usual, but didn't say more than a few words to anyone. In fact, during the day, two or three people asked me if I was feeling ill. I said that I was fine, just thinking about a difficult work problem. That evening I left the office at six o'clock. I walked quickly to the street where I had first seen the man. Soon I found the door; it was number 7 Felka utca. While I waited, I looked at the street carefully. It was short and dark, and there was still a lot of snow around from yesterday. On either side of the street were blocks of flats which had been built in the late nineteenth and early twentieth centuries. Most of them were dirty and in bad condition. On many of them you could still see the holes the gunshots had made during the fighting in World War II or the 1956 revolution. The blocks were all five floors high with big front doors. At this time on a winter evening only one or two kitchen windows were lit as people made their evening meals.

I waited, walking slowly up and down. It was cold. I felt a bit like a private detective in an American film. A few people walked along the street, but mainly it was as quiet as it had been the night before. As the time got near, I stood opposite the entrance to number 7 with the wall behind my back. Nothing happened. At seven o'clock, a woman with a small dog came along the street and went in through the door, but then there was nothing to see. And there was certainly nobody like myself there.

I went over to the door of number 7, and looked at the names beside the bells for each flat. I don't know what I expected to find. But there were just the usual Hungarian family names, and a couple of small companies that had offices on the ground floor of the building.

Then I walked to the bar where I'd gone the night before. I walked along Felka utca, crossed the road and went into Gergely utca. I found the bar, and went down the steps and into the smoky room. I ordered a red wine. The barman looked at me.

'Did you find your friend, then?' he asked

I was surprised. 'I'm sorry?' I replied, coughing into my wine.

'The man you were looking for last night,' he said. 'Did you find him?'

'No, I'm afraid I didn't,' I answered. 'That's why I'm here, really. I was hoping I might see him tonight.'

'What's he like then, this friend of yours?' asked the barman.

'Well, he's . . . er . . . he's . . . ' I stopped. The barman looked at me, waiting. 'He looks very much like me, actually.'

'I can't say that I've seen anyone like you here,' he said. 'But then I only bought the place six weeks ago, so I don't really know everyone who comes in here yet. Just the usual people who are in here now.'

A man came up to the bar, and I moved away, watching the end of the news on the television and drinking my wine. I looked at the people in the room – they all looked just like those I'd seen the night before. But there was no-one like me. I decided to leave.

When I got home I was pleased to find a note from Andrea on the kitchen table. It said that she was out teaching a new student – so I didn't have to make up any more stories about where I'd been.

*   *   *

That night I had a strange dream. In my dream, I heard the noise of a door shutting loudly. I was running out of a building and I ran into someone. A man. He fell down. I turned to say sorry. I saw that it was me lying on the ground. I woke up feeling afraid and cold in the dark, although the bedroom was nice and warm. The strange thing was that it was as if the dream had changed everything round: because in the dream it was *me* who ran out of the building, not the man, and when I looked at the man on the ground it was myself.

Suddenly, Andrea woke up.

'What's the matter, love?' she asked sleepily, turning on the light.

15

I couldn't speak at first. She sat up and looked at me.

'You look bad,' she said. She sounded worried. 'Do you feel ill?'

'No,' I started. 'No. It was . . . just . . . just a dream.'

'Poor darling,' she said, holding my head and kissing me on the cheek. 'Come on, let's try and get some sleep.'

I lay down again. She turned off the light and soon went back to sleep. But I lay there in bed, looking at the four walls in the dark, watching the dream over and over again in the cinema inside my head.

I felt afraid, but I didn't really understand what it was that I was afraid of.

Chapter 5 *I tell Andrea*

And so my new life began. Every day that week I went to work, every night I waited outside the house at number 7 Felka utca, and then I spent time in the bar. And every night I had the same dream and woke up feeling afraid in the dark. And if I went back to sleep, I had the dream again. And if I didn't go back to sleep, I lay in bed in the dark trying to understand what was happening to me. And every morning I was more and more tired, and I wasn't nice to Andrea. I felt terrible because of the dreams and because I was so tired. And I felt worse because Andrea didn't know why I was arriving late every evening, and I didn't tell her the truth.

Things at work became difficult. I couldn't think about the important things I had to do. And even worse, the next day I argued with Andrea. She couldn't understand why I had to go to the Gergely utca bar every night, and of course I felt I couldn't tell her. And then because I didn't feel good, I started drinking more than the two glasses of wine I had had the first two nights.

I started staying in the bar much longer because I was afraid to go home and try to sleep. I was afraid to dream the same dream. On Thursday, when I came home very late after drinking too much, Andrea had already gone to bed.

On Friday, I was late home again, but when I got in Andrea was waiting up for me. She looked very unhappy.

Her face was white and her pretty blue eyes were red. She had been crying.

'John,' she said, as I got some bread and cheese to eat, 'what is the matter?'

I said nothing as I ate.

'John,' she tried again, 'you must tell me what's happened. You've changed completely. Please . . . talk to me.'

I looked up at her, this wonderful woman I loved so much, and saw how much I was hurting her. I felt so terrible that I started crying.

She put her arms around me and talked to me quietly, as if I were a little child. Then she took my face between her hands.

'Tell me, darling,' she said quietly. 'I want to help you.'

And so I told her everything. The words came out quickly, and when I'd finished she suddenly laughed and laughed.

'It's not funny,' I said angrily.

'No, darling,' she answered. 'It's not funny at all, but I feel so happy.' She stopped laughing, and continued in a serious voice. 'You see, I thought you'd found somebody else. Another woman.'

After that we held each other and kissed for a very long time. Then she made me tell her the story again, very slowly. She kept asking questions, trying to get all the information about every part of it.

'Right,' she said. 'Tomorrow is Saturday, and neither of us is working. We'll go round to number 7 Felka utca and start asking some questions. I'm sure there's a very easy answer to this story.'

I felt so happy. She was so sweet and good and I was sure that everything was going to be all right.

Chapter 6 *Talking to the housekeepers*

The next day was very sunny, though still very cold. The strong sunshine made me feel more hopeful about the future, now that I had told Andrea about what had happened. I finally felt good after an excellent night's sleep – it was the first time I hadn't dreamt about meeting myself for nearly a week.

At ten o'clock we walked round to Felka utca. I was really pleased that Andrea was with me; although my Hungarian was good, she would be able to talk to people much more easily than me.

The first person we spoke to was the housekeeper – the lady who had the small ground-floor flat near the door in return for doing jobs in the building, such as cleaning the stairs and checking the lift and the lights.

We asked her a lot of questions. When we asked if there was anybody who looked like me living in the flats she looked at me for a long time, and then said there wasn't. Andrea next asked her how long she'd worked there; the answer was twenty-one years. And did she know everybody? She did. And were there any new families? There weren't. And were there any men looking like me who'd lived here and then moved away lately? There weren't. We thanked her, and left.

Out in the street, we looked at each other. I was starting to think I must be imagining everything.

'Perhaps it was a visitor,' said Andrea, realising how bad I felt.

'Or perhaps,' I said, 'perhaps he lives in the other building, where the bar is, and I didn't see where he went.'

'Maybe,' said Andrea. 'Let's go and try.'

We walked round to Gergely utca and stopped outside the bar.

'So,' she said, looking down the steps to the cellar, 'this is where you've been spending your evenings!'

My face went red. 'Sorry,' I said.

'I'm joking, love!' she said laughing. 'Look – the main entrance to the block of flats is next door. It would have been easy for you to mistake which one he went into in the dark and snow.'

'Yes, you're right,' I answered.

But I kept thinking about the fact that there had been no footprints in the snow.

Inside the building we met another housekeeper. This time it was a man in his fifties who'd worked there for twelve years. We asked the same questions as we had asked before, and got the same answers. He'd never seen anyone there who looked like me.

I felt very bad after these second answers. I thought that Andrea would think there was something wrong with me. Andrea took my hand.

'Come on,' she said, laughing. 'Let's go and have a drink in your famous bar!'

I was so surprised that I didn't have time to say anything as I followed her down the steps.

The barman welcomed me with a friendly smile and

a joke about good friends bringing more friends. I introduced him to Andrea, then we took our wine and stood in a corner and talked about what had happened.

'There is one important thing about all of this, Andrea,' I said when we seemed to have talked about it all. 'And I know it sounds very strange, but I don't think this person just looked like me. I think it *was* me.'

I'd said this to her before when I'd told her the first time, and she'd laughed and said it was impossible. But I had a feeling deep inside me that I was right.

'But, John,' she asked, 'how could that be?'

'I don't know, love,' I replied. 'I just feel it. So perhaps we shouldn't be looking for someone who lives in these buildings now. Perhaps we should be looking for someone who, well . . . er . . . someone who's dead. And who *I* am now.'

Andrea looked at me very hard.

'John,' she said, 'I've never heard you say anything like this before. What do you mean?'

'I wish I knew what I meant,' I said with difficulty. 'All I know is that I have a strange idea inside my head that tells me these things are possible.'

We finished our drink without speaking and left.

'Andrea,' I said as we walked home, 'you must believe me. I need your help to try and understand what's happened to me.'

'I'm trying to believe you, love,' she answered, turning to look at me. 'It's just that it's very difficult to understand.'

'It's difficult for me, too,' I said.

Chapter 7 *Doppelgänger*

After that Saturday my life returned to what it had been, in one way. I went back to work on Monday and I was my old self, and things went well. I didn't have the dreams at night any more. And I didn't visit Felka utca and the bar every night either, although I still went in once or twice a week.

But there were also big changes. The next Wednesday Andrea came home from a visit to the doctor's with big news: she was expecting a baby! We were extremely happy. We had often talked about starting a family, but hadn't thought it would happen quite so soon. And then the day after that she lost her biggest teaching job – fifteen hours a week with an international bank. They didn't want to pay for Hungarian lessons for the people who worked there any more. The ups and downs of life!

A week or so later I told Zsolt – the wine cellar barman – that Andrea had lost her most important job. He said he was looking for someone to help him in the bar. He said it wasn't a job for an 'intelligent lady' like my wife, but he also said he could offer her good money, and he felt the place needed a woman's touch to make it better.

I talked about the offer with Andrea, and in the end she took the job. The pay wasn't as good as for teaching, but the bar was very close to home. Also, she didn't have to spend hours working on her lessons like she did for teaching. And she soon made quite a difference to the bar.

When I went in the week after she'd started it looked much better – there were flowers on the bar, and pictures on the walls.

'I've asked Zsolt if we can make one side of the bar into a sitting area with tables and chairs,' Andrea told me over dinner one evening, 'and he's agreed.'

'Why do you want to do that?' I asked.

'Well, I thought more people might want to come in,' she said. 'And women might like it, too.'

And she was right. Soon after that women started going to the bar as well as men. Zsolt was very pleased.

However, between all these new things in our life, I didn't forget my strange meeting with 'myself'. I started doing lots of reading about life after death. It was a completely new thing for me, and I found it very interesting. I learnt many things I didn't know. Perhaps the most interesting thing I found out was that what had happened to me has a name:

DOPPELGÄNGER: A German word which is used in English. It means something like 'double-walker' or 'double-goer' – a ghostly double of a living person, who comes to give messages about danger or to offer advice. It can only be seen by its 'owner'. (This was why there were no footprints, and why Zsolt had seen nothing in the bar, I thought.)

However, it can sometimes be seen by somebody close if it has an important message. It is usually thought to bring bad luck, and is often believed to show that there will soon be a serious problem or a death.

I showed Andrea the page from the book I was reading.

'And so is this what you think you saw?' she asked, looking surprised.

'Well, it sounds like it, doesn't it?' I answered.

So now I knew – I had met my doppelgänger. The next question was why?

Chapter 8   *A holiday*

In August Andrea gave up working for Zsolt. We spent my summer holiday happily painting a small room in our flat so that it was ready for the baby, and on 16 September our daughter was born. We gave her the name Kati. After that, things changed even more as we got used to all the differences a new baby makes to her parents' lives. It was hard work, but we were very happy. And I was so busy that for a while I forgot about what had happened in Felka utca.

We decided to go to England at Christmas. We wanted my parents and family to meet Kati, and this was a good chance. We soon learnt how difficult it is to go on holiday with a small baby. You need to take so many things! It took us a very long time to get ready.

We flew from Budapest to London Heathrow on 22 December. My parents met us and drove us to their house in a village near Swindon, about an hour from the airport. Everyone was very happy. It was only the third time that Andrea had visited my parents' place, and only her second English Christmas. And this time we had a new baby in the family with us. Of course, Kati was the centre of everyone's attention. The next day, my mother said she would look after Kati so that Andrea and I could go into Swindon to do some Christmas shopping. The town was very colourful, with lights and Christmas trees everywhere. And it was very busy, with all the shops full of people buying

Christmas presents. We enjoyed ourselves, and got some more presents to add to the special Hungarian Christmas things we had brought with us.

That evening, my father was out at his office Christmas dinner and Andrea was tired after our day in town, so I decided to go down to the village pub and see if any of my old friends were there. I saw one or two neighbours and talked to them for a while, but none of my good friends were there. I was just going to leave when in walked Paul Harris.

Paul had been one of my closest friends at school, but he hadn't been in the village the last few times I'd visited my parents. He was a journalist and had lived in many different places since we'd left school.

'Paul!' I called, as he walked into the bar.

'John!' he said. 'How good to see you!'

'Good to see you, too,' I replied. 'I was just leaving. None of our old friends are here.'

'No,' he said sadly. 'Most of them have left – gone to other places for work or wives!'

'What would you like to drink?' I asked.

'I'll have a pint of bitter, please, John,' he replied.

We took our beer to a quiet corner of the pub and started to tell each other our news.

'Just back to have Christmas with the family,' he explained.

'On your own?' I said, asking myself what had happened to his wife, Liz.

'I'm afraid so,' he said, looking down at his beer. 'Liz left me last summer.'

'I'm sorry, Paul,' I replied. 'I had no idea . . . '

'Don't worry,' he said. 'The worst part is over. So tell me about you. My mother told me there's a baby now . . . '

And so I told him all about Kati, and Andrea, and life in Budapest. And after a couple more beers I told him about meeting myself.

Paul was one of my oldest and best friends, and I knew he would take the story seriously.

'That's very interesting, John,' he said when I'd finished. He didn't laugh or tell me I was stupid. He seemed to be thinking about something. 'There was a story about the same thing – doppelgängers, and people meeting themselves – in one of the magazines I write for.'

'Did you read it?' I asked, hoping he might have some more information.

'Only the first part,' he said. 'But I remember it said that this happens to quite a lot of people everywhere.'

'Well, that's good news,' I replied. 'I thought I was going crazy or something!'

'No, John, you're not,' he said, smiling. 'But you should be careful. I remember that it also said that bad things had happened to many people after seeing a doppelgänger.'

'Yes, I read that, too,' I said. 'In a book in Budapest. But anyway, it's good to know I'm not alone.'

'Yes, that may help you to feel happier,' he said seriously. 'But I remember one story from the magazine where the doppelgänger was trying to tell a woman not to drive her son to school one day. She didn't understand and that same day they had a car accident and her son was killed.'

'Oh, really!' I said, surprised.

'So perhaps you should be careful,' said Paul.

'I will, don't worry,' I answered.

In one way I felt much happier knowing that what had happened to me was not so unusual, but I started trying to understand what kind of message my doppelgänger was trying to bring me. Thinking about it made me feel uncomfortable, so I tried to forget it and enjoy Christmas. But it wasn't very easy.

The rest of the Christmas holiday in England passed quickly. We ate lots of nice food, played family games, visited friends and family in other places, and really enjoyed ourselves. Soon it was time to go back to Hungary.

We flew back on 29 December, returning to spend New Year with Andrea's family in the snowy Hungarian countryside. Perhaps it was because we couldn't go out much and there wasn't much to do except sit around the house, but I started thinking about my doppelgänger story more and more. I was trying to decide what the meeting with myself had meant. Andrea said that I wasn't joining in with family things much. But when I told her why, she got angry with me, and we argued.

'I thought you'd forgotten about that stupid story,' she said.

'I've tried to, Andrea,' I answered, 'but it keeps coming back to me.'

'Well, it had better go away from you very quickly!' she answered. 'I want a man who looks after his family, talks to his wife and plays with his daughter. I don't want someone who sits around the house all day looking into space.' And she walked out of the room.

I understood that Andrea was tired and wanted me to

pay more attention to my family, and I tried to be better, but then two days later we went home. I went back to work as usual on Monday 5 January.

Chapter 9   *The date gets closer again*

At three o'clock in the morning on 11 January I suddenly sat up in bed. I listened. Kati wasn't crying (in fact, she usually slept all through the night by then).

But I was cold and afraid in the dark.

Suddenly, I realised what had happened. I had had the dream again. The street. The door. Me running out. The man on the ground. Me. Meeting myself.

I felt terrible. Since little Kati had entered my life, I hadn't had the bad dreams. I thought they were a thing of the past, but here they were again, as big and black as before.

I couldn't sleep, so I went into the kitchen and made myself some tea. Then I went to the bookshelf in the living room and took down last year's diary. You see, I always keep a diary where I write down what happens each day. Monday 18 January was when I'd had the strange meeting last year. It was seven days until that date now.

Then suddenly, a new idea came into my head: it was the date that was important! It all seemed so clear! It was not surprising that I'd never met myself again on all those evenings I'd waited in Felka utca! I needed to be there on 18 January. Next Sunday evening. And I'd had the dream again to make me remember!

I walked up and down again and again, with thoughts running quickly through my head. It was the date that was important. My reading about ghosts and life after death had helped me to find out about doppelgängers, but I still didn't understand. What I needed to do was to find out what had happened in Felka utca or Gergely utca one 18 January in the past.

*   *   *

The six days which followed that night were very difficult.

The next morning, I told Andrea that I'd had the dream again.

'I think it's the date – 18 January – which must be important,' I said. Andrea carried on giving Kati her milk.

'I want to do some reading about it,' I went on. 'I'd like to start looking at some old newspapers to find out what happened there on 18 January. Where can I go to find old newspapers in Budapest?'

Andrea was angry with me.

'Leave it alone, John!' she shouted. 'There are more important things in your life now!'

'But Andrea . . . ' I started.

'You've got a baby to look after,' she continued. 'And me. You can't use your free time looking for something you won't be able to find!'

Kati started to cry. It seemed that she understood that her mother and father were unhappy.

I decided to tell Andrea everything I was thinking and doing this time; it had been no good keeping the truth from her last year. So on Friday 16 January, after having the dream every night that week, I talked to her about the coming Sunday.

'Andrea, I have to go to Felka utca on Sunday,' I started. She said nothing. 'And I'd like you to come with me . . . '

'You must be joking!' she said.

'But listen, love,' I went on, taking her hand, 'I *need* you to come with me.'

'How would that help you?' she asked, taking her hand away.

'There are two reasons,' I continued. 'First, because I'm afraid to go by myself, and second, because I want to know if you see anything.'

'But how do you know that this man will be there?' she asked.

'I don't,' I replied. 'But it's the only idea I have about what happened – that it's the date which is important.'

Andrea said nothing. I watched her.

'Please, love,' I said. 'It would help me a lot.'

'But what about Kati?' she asked. 'I'm not taking her with me.'

'Of course not,' I said, happier. 'We'll get your friend Petra to look after her.'

She said nothing again.

'Yes?' I asked, carefully. She sat thinking for a long time. I waited.

'All right,' she said. 'But this really is the last time.'

'OK,' I said. 'OK. But . . . thank you.'

I was very pleased, and went to telephone Petra at once. Petra was an old friend of Andrea's who sometimes looked after Kati when we went out. I told her we'd unexpectedly been invited to tea at my boss's flat. Luckily, she said yes.

I hoped that I would sleep better knowing Andrea was coming with me on Sunday. I didn't. I had the dream again and again that night and on Saturday.

The dream was almost the same, except that I now

33

seemed to hear a loud noise in the street just before the man came out of the door. I tried to understand what the loud noise was. I listened in my dream, but it wasn't very clear. I knew it was something important, something that would help me, but I couldn't be sure what it was. I often woke up after the dream and felt afraid. I stayed awake in the dark trying to decide what the dream was trying to tell me. I also worried about what was going to happen if I met my doppelgänger again on Sunday.

Chapter 10 *18 January*

Sunday started very quietly. We didn't talk much to each other. Both Andrea and I were unsure of what we were going to do and what might happen.

At three o'clock on Sunday afternoon, Petra arrived to look after Kati.

'What's the matter with you two?' she asked, as we put our coats on. 'You look as if you're visiting someone in hospital rather than going to a tea party!'

We tried to smile as we left the house, but we were both afraid.

We had decided to go to for a walk to use the time before our meeting. We went to Margaret Island – the lovely island park in the middle of the River Danube. It was a place we always liked going to, with its huge trees full of singing birds. We often took Kati there to get some fresh air. But today, although it was quite a nice winter afternoon, we were thinking about the meeting too much to enjoy it. We didn't speak much. At quarter to six we started to walk back over the wide grey river and into the streets of the Thirteenth District.

By half past six we were standing opposite number 7 Felka utca. It was evening by now, and the street was as dark as usual.

'Where do you think we should wait?' asked Andrea.

'You stay on this side of the road,' I answered. 'When it's

time, I'll go and stand outside the door. You watch and listen carefully.'

At ten to seven I walked across the road. There was nobody around, just Andrea and I.

Then suddenly I heard a noise, then an inside door shut. I looked across at Andrea. I heard the sound of someone running. The door opened and out ran a man, straight into me. I fell to the ground, shouting, 'Hey . . . !' The man looked round. He had my face.

'Sorry,' he said in Hungarian, and went off quickly to the end of the street. I stood up. Andrea was standing there looking at me. I could see she didn't understand what had just happened.

'Quick!' I shouted. 'Follow him!'

I ran up to the end of the street, and crossed over into Gergely utca. The man was just going down into the wine bar. Andrea arrived by my side a moment later.

'There!' I shouted. 'Did you see? He went down into the wine cellar. Come on!'

I ran along to Zsolt's bar, pulling Andrea after me. I went down the stairs and pushed the door. It was shut. Of course, it was Sunday afternoon, Zsolt's afternoon off. I sat down on the steps and looked at the locked door. Andrea sat beside me and put her arm round my shoulder.

When I looked at her she had a strange look in her eyes.

As we walked home we talked about what had happened.

'It was just the same as last year,' I said. 'Just the same.'

'But I saw nothing and heard nothing. All I saw was you falling over and shouting,' she said. 'And it was very strange – you just fell over.'

We walked the rest of the way home without speaking. When Petra had left, we didn't talk very much all evening. For me, everything had been the same as last year. Except that this time there had been no snow to show that the man had left no footprints, and the bar he went into had been closed.

That night I had the dream again.

I was standing outside the building. I heard the new noise – much louder now. The door opened. The man ran out of the door and knocked me over. He turned to say sorry, and when I looked at him it was *me* I saw. The strange thing was that every time I had the dream the noise got louder and louder. And I always woke up feeling terribly afraid.

Chapter 11   *A little bit of history*

The next Monday there was no important new work to do for a few days, so I asked my boss for some time off work. I told him Andrea wasn't feeling well and needed some help at home with the baby in the afternoons. He kindly said I could go to the office only in the mornings, for a week or two until the next big piece of work arrived from Britain. I decided not to tell Andrea what I was going to do. She had been kind enough to come with me to the meeting that Sunday when she really didn't want to, and I didn't want to make her angry or worried again.

At two o'clock in the afternoon on Monday 19 January, I was sitting in the reading room of the Budapest City Library with a lot of big books in front of me. They were not really books, but newspapers that had been made into books. I wanted to find out everything that had happened in Budapest's Thirteenth District on every 18 January. I decided to read one of Hungary's best-known newspapers, because it always had lots of news about what was happening in Budapest. I had asked the librarian for this newspaper for every month of January, starting from ten years before.

I went through the Budapest pages for each year very carefully. I studied the days between 12 and 25 January, as this was the week before and the week after the date of meeting my doppelgänger. Of course, I was always very careful when I got to each 18 January. It took me longer than I'd expected, and I was only just able to finish the first ten Januarys before the library closed at five o'clock. My Hungarian was good, but it still took me a long time to read the old newspapers.

I went to the reading room each afternoon. I discovered all sorts of things I never knew about Budapest. Much of what I read about from before 1990 was, of course, about the Communist Party. There was more and more information about groups of politicians and workers who visited from other Eastern European countries, the deeper into the past I went.

I sometimes found information about the Thirteenth District, but nothing interesting, and I had found nothing about Felka utca.

I was beginning to think I would never find anything, or that my reading would have to go back into the nineteenth century. On Saturday I told Andrea that I had a meeting at work, but instead I went to the library at half past eight in the morning, with a complete day ahead of me. By early afternoon I had got back to the 1940s.

It was almost closing time when I reached 19 January 1945. By now I was tired, but then I saw something at the bottom of the Budapest page of the newspaper. It jumped out at me. It said in Hungarian:

YOUNG MOTHER AND CHILD KILLED AS FIGHTING ENDS IN PEST

The story said that the day before (18 January!) was the end of the fighting between the German soldiers inside Pest and the Russians who were all around them. It then said that the happy day for Pest was also sad for people in the Thirteenth District: a Russian bomb had hit a Gergely utca building; it didn't explode, but it destroyed the cellar, killing a young mother and her daughter. The dead woman was later named as Mrs Szabó.

I made a copy of this story and went home. I decided to tell Andrea about what I had found out.

*　　*　　*

'And where have you been?' Andrea asked as I walked into the flat.

'What do you mean?' I asked back.

'I rang you at the office to tell you I was taking Kati out this afternoon,' she replied. 'The receptionist said you weren't there, and she also said that there was no meeting.' Andrea was very angry.

I looked at the floor.

'Well, John?' she went on. 'Where was it this time? Felka utca? Gergely utca? Some other stupid street?'

'Andrea,' I started, 'I've been reading the newspapers.' I took out the copy of the newspaper story. 'Look,' I said.

She read it quickly.

'And what do you think this shows?' she asked. She looked angry.

'Well, the date,' I said, 'and the street. They're the same. 18 January and Gergely utca.'

'So, what are you going to do now?' she replied.

'Well, we must try to find somebody from this Mrs Szabó's family, I think,' I replied. 'Perhaps they still live in the building.'

'Don't say "we",' she said. 'I told you that last Sunday

was my last time. And anyway, which building: Gergely utca or Felka utca?'

'I don't know,' I answered. 'But just think about it. My doppelgänger comes out of the building in Felka utca and runs round to Gergely utca on 18 January. Perhaps the people were hiding from the fighting in his house. He was visiting a friend. He heard about it, and ran home to see what had happened. So he lived in Gergely utca.'

'You're very good at telling stories, John,' said Andrea, and walked into the bedroom.

'But, Andrea,' I said, following her, 'I've got to find out, don't you understand? If I don't, I'll never be free of this dream! I have to know the truth. It could be important for me in some way. There has to be a reason for this meeting.'

'Look, John,' she said. 'You do what you want, but just don't expect any help from me. Do you understand?'

And with that she picked up Kati, who was already dressed to go out, put on her coat and walked out of the flat.

Chapter 12 *Looking for the truth*

I stood looking at the closed door and listened as Andrea took the lift down to the ground floor. I tried to decide what to do. I knew Andrea was tired of the doppelgänger story, and so was I. And I knew she wanted me to spend more time with her and Kati, and so did I. But I needed to know why this was happening to me.

After a few minutes, I put my coat back on and walked round to Gergely utca, and met the housekeeper again. This time I had to do the talking. I asked lots of questions. Was there a family called Szabó in any of the flats? No. Had there ever been a family called Szabó in the time she'd been housekeeper? No. Were there any old people living in the building? Only Mrs Kovacs on the second floor, who was probably in her seventies. I decided to try her.

She was a very nice old lady, but she had only moved into the flat in 1979 when her husband had died, so she could be closer to her daughter and family who lived nearby.

After that, I walked round to 7 Felka utca and found the housekeeper. I asked her the same questions, and I was very happy when she told me that there *was* a Szabó family on the third floor!

I took the lift up, and found the flat. The door was answered by a big man wearing a dirty vest.

'Mr Szabó?' I asked, feeling rather unsure of myself.

'Who wants to know?' he answered, looking angry.

'I'm . . . er . . . trying to find part of my wife's family called Szabó,' I said, thinking quickly. 'I . . . er . . . want to know if you can help me.'

'What do you want to know?' he asked, in an ugly voice.

'Did your family live in this flat at the end of the war?' I asked.

'It's none of your business,' he replied, starting to shut the door.

'Oh please, Mr Szabó,' I said. 'I've come a long way, and it's very important for me to find out.'

'Look,' said Mr Szabó, 'how do I know you're not the police, or a detective or something?'

'Mr Szabó, look at me,' I replied. 'I'm English. I work with computers. I only need to know if your family lived here during the war.'

He seemed to become a little softer.

'No. My parents moved here after the revolution in 1956,' he said. 'They're dead now. I was born here in 1958. OK?'

'Oh, I see,' I answered. 'Thank you so much for your time.'

What a horrible man, I thought as I walked back to the lift. And what's more, not the right man!

I went back down to the housekeeper.

'Not the right Szabós, I'm afraid,' I said when she came to the door.

'Oh dear,' said the lady. 'I'm sorry, but we haven't got any more!'

'But are there any old people?' I asked. 'Or are there any families who have lived here for a very long time?'

'Yes,' she answered. 'There is one person: old Mrs Fischer on the fourth floor. She's been here for ages.'

'Oh, wonderful,' I replied with a smile. 'Thank you.'

I got back into the lift and went up to the fourth floor and found the right flat.

I had to ring the bell again and again before the old lady opened the door. She couldn't hear very well. But she let me into her small kitchen, and offered me a cup of coffee.

'Mrs Fischer, how long have you lived here in Felka utca?' I had to repeat each question about three times before she understood what I said, because of my Hungarian and her hearing problems.

'Since 1937, my dear,' she replied. 'I moved into this flat as a young wife with my new husband Pál. He died five years ago.'

'I'm sorry,' I said. 'Did you live here during the war?'

'Yes, we did,' she answered. 'Well, *I* did. My husband was away fighting most of the time.'

'Were you here in 1945, when the Russians got the Germans out of Pest?' I asked.

'Yes, I most certainly was,' Mrs Fischer replied. 'We didn't know who were worse – the Germans or the Russians!'

'And can you remember any of the other people who lived in this building then?' I continued.

'Well, some of them,' she said. 'Lots of people were killed.' Here she seemed to lose herself thinking about those bad days again.

'Perhaps you remember a family called Szabó?' I asked.

She looked at me with a very strange face. I thought she

was going to say that she remembered nothing, when suddenly she said very quietly, 'Poor, poor János.'

I looked at the old lady and waited.

'Would you like some more coffee, or a glass of juice, perhaps?' she said, standing up.

'No, that's fine, thank you, Mrs Fischer,' I said. 'I'm sorry, but what were you saying about János Szabó a moment ago?'

Again I waited.

'Oh, it was terrible,' she said. 'We were all so sorry for him. It was such a bad thing to happen. And right on the day when the fighting ended here in Pest.'

She stopped again. I waited, thoughts running through my head.

'He had looked after his family all through the war,' she said. 'His health was not very good, and so he didn't go away to fight. Then in 1943 his wife had a baby. A sweet little girl. They were so happy.'

I smiled, thinking of my Kati.

'His wife used to go and help in a shop in a cellar,' she continued. 'Then on that day . . . '

'But where was the cellar shop?' I asked quickly.

'Oh, not far,' she replied. 'Just round the corner in Gergely utca.'

I looked at her very hard. I couldn't believe what I was hearing.

'And on that day – the day when the fighting stopped – in January 1945,' went on the old lady, 'János was down in the courtyard, the small outdoor area where children played. He was talking to a few of us neighbours. We knew the fighting was nearly over. You could just hear a few guns from outside and sometimes a bomb coming in from the Russians. Suddenly, a man ran into our building shouting for János, telling him to go to the Gergely utca cellar shop quickly: something had happened. He ran out immediately. And when he came back he had changed completely.'

Here she stopped again for a long time.

'Can you tell me what had happened, Mrs Fischer?' I asked, quietly.

'Oh, it was too bad,' she said, her eyes wet with crying. 'It was such bad luck, so unfair, after all that war. A Russian bomb hit the building above the cellar shop in Gergely utca. It didn't explode, but it was heavy enough to destroy the cellar. And so that poor young woman and the baby were killed. So unfair.'

I looked at the old lady feeling both happy and sad. I had finally found out the truth from someone who had been there.

'What happened to János after that?' I asked.

'Oh, the poor, *poor* man!' said the old lady. 'He was never the same again. He stopped wanting to live. In the end he died fighting in the streets in 1956. We all thought he wanted to die. He had nothing left to live for.'

Chapter 13 *Problems at home*

I'm not sure how I walked back to our flat. I was terribly worried. Andrea came home with Kati at eight o'clock, and put her to bed, I wanted to tell Andrea what had happened. But I didn't know what to say because she had been so angry about it that afternoon. I also wanted to talk about what I had been told. I was both very interested and afraid at the same time.

'Andrea,' I started, 'I've found out what happened.'

She didn't answer; she was looking at a newspaper.

'Andrea,' I tried again, 'would you like me to tell you what I've found out?'

She looked at me coldly.

'Look, John,' she said, 'you know that I've really had enough of this story of yours, but I expect I'll have to hear the next part. Go on.' She looked very tired and worried.

I told her what Mrs Fischer had said quickly and quietly. She looked at me as I talked. When I had finished she said, 'And so what?'

'Well, don't you understand – it's him I see every 18 January,' I replied.

'Who?' asked Andrea.

'János Szabó, of course,' I said.

'Oh, John!' she said. 'How can you see a dead man? I really think you must be ill.'

'What do you mean?' I asked.

'I mean that you're probably very tired from work, and

because of the baby,' she went on, 'and that you need some help from a doctor.'

'But, Andrea,' I shouted, 'you came with me on 18 January and saw what happened . . . '

'John, remember that all I saw was you falling over and shouting,' she said.

I sat looking at her without saying anything. My wife didn't believe me. She thought that I was ill. And yet I knew it was all true. This man – János Szabó – my doppelgänger – was there for a reason. He was there to tell me something, to help me in some way.

Over the next few weeks, I often tried to talk about it with Andrea, but she never wanted to listen to me. Sadly, my doppelgänger seemed to be building a wall between us – talking to each other became much more difficult than it had been before. We often spent evenings without talking much, or my wife went to bed early, saying she was tired after a day looking after Kati, and I stayed up watching old films on the TV until the early hours of the morning.

I thought about it carefully, again and again. Some things were true facts. A man called János Szabó had lived at number 7 Felka utca. On 18 January 1945 his wife and daughter had been killed in the cellar that was now Zsolt's bar in Gergely utca. Other things were difficult to understand: I had been outside the Felka utca building twice on the anniversary of that date – 18 January – and I had met the man. And he looked the same as me. What did it all mean?

Chapter 14 *Another year goes by*

The year passed very quickly. Andrea and I still lived in the same flat; we slept in the same bed and ate the same food. We both took care of our beautiful little girl, but really we weren't very close any more. It was as if János Szabó stood between us. I spent longer at work each day and quite often worked on Saturdays, too. I usually had a glass of wine at Zsolt's bar on two or three evenings a week. On two evenings a week Andrea went out to yoga classes.

Then things slowly started to change. We had a very good time when we took Kati for her second visit to England in August. England was so far away from Budapest, and there were so many things to see and do, and so many friends and family to visit that I was able to forget about my meetings with myself.

Of course, everyone loved Kati – she was such a pretty, happy little girl – and this seemed to help Andrea and I to build our love for each other again. Perhaps the best moment of the summer was when we took Kati to the sea for the first time. She loved playing in the water and on the beach, and we enjoyed playing with her.

After we came back from our holiday in September things seemed better at home, too. I began some very important work which took much more of my time. Andrea decided she wanted to start working again, so we put Kati into a very nice school for small children. It was just mornings at first, but the little girl liked it so much that in November we let her stay all day. Andrea taught a few Hungarian lessons here and there and also helped Zsolt in his bar again for a couple of mornings a week. It seemed as if our problems had gone away.

We spent the Christmas holidays at home on our own, as a happy little family. Then for New Year we went to the country to stay with Andrea's family, as usual. We had a very good time there, as well.

It was only when I went back to work on 6 January, and I started looking at dates for finishing the work I was doing, that I suddenly realised that it would soon be 18 January again. I very much wanted to talk to Andrea about it, but I was afraid of destroying the happiness we had found again.

As if to make me remember what had happened on 18 January the last two years, I had a terrible dream. It was really the same dream – the door in Felka utca, the loud noise from somewhere near, the man running out, me falling onto the ground and the man running off down the street. I followed him, and this time I watched him as he started looking for something in the destroyed cellar in Gergely utca.

Suddenly, I woke up and shouted out, 'Help me!' I was crying and hot. I felt terrible.

Andrea woke up. 'What is it, John?' she asked. She looked really afraid.

I looked at her, and pulled her very close to me. I had a horrible feeling that this dream and the meetings with myself had something to do with her.

Chapter 15   *I discover some more facts*

The next day, I was walking home from work. Of course, I was asking myself if I should go to meet my doppelgänger, János Szabó, for the third time on 18 January.

As I went along a street I saw some men putting up a new sign on an old shop. There was the owner's name in red, and below it the word *Szabó* in green. In the window there were suits, jackets and trousers. *Szabó*. Tailor. The tailor's was getting a new sign. '*Szabó*,' I thought. Then I said 'János Szabó' out loud. Then I thought, 'János the tailor. John the tailor. John Taylor.' I stopped in the street. János Szabó was John Taylor! My doppelgänger and I shared a name. John Taylor was the English for the Hungarian János Szabó. My hair stood up. Here was something new and important: we shared the same name!

I needed a drink, so I went into Zsolt's bar and thought about what I had discovered. I tried to decide what to do. Should I tell Andrea about this? Perhaps it would help her to believe me? I didn't know. I remembered the man in my new dream last night, in the destroyed cellar, looking for something. I decided to go and see Mrs Fischer again.

I walked quickly round to Felka utca and went inside and up to her flat.

'Do you remember I came to ask you about János Szabó, Mrs Fischer?' I asked when she let me in.

'Oh, the poor young man,' she said, looking at me

sadly. 'And do you know something – you look *so* like him, too.'

This was quite a surprise. 'Really?' I asked.

'Come here under the light,' she said.

I moved under the strong light in the hall.

'Yes,' she said, looking at me carefully. 'You look very much the same. The eyes, the nose, the mouth. Very much the same. I didn't look at you carefully when you came last time. Oh, the poor young man.'

I felt myself getting very hot.

'Mrs Fischer, I came to ask you something different,' I said. Then I went on very slowly, because I was so afraid of her possible answer. 'Can you remember the names of the wife and daughter who were killed in the cellar?'

'Well, I know the wife was called Andrea,' she started, and I felt my face go white, 'but as for the little girl . . . let's think . . . '

I waited for a moment. She didn't seem able to remember.

'It wasn't . . . ' I waited, and then said, 'It wasn't Kati, was it?'

Mrs Fischer looked at me and smiled. 'Yes, that was it,' she said. 'Quite right. Andrea and Kati. The poor young things.'

I thanked her and left as quickly as I could. My head was turning round and round. I felt sick. Outside in the cold street, I stood against the wall of the building. There were too many new things inside my head to understand at once: my doppelgänger had the same name as me – Szabó, or Taylor – I looked like him, and his wife *and* daughter had the same names as mine!

I started to ask myself how many other things about our lives were the same. The next week I went to the Public Records Office in my lunch break. This is the office where they keep information about everyone who lives in Hungary today, and also about people who lived there in the past. I asked for information about János Szabó who had lived in Felka utca in 1945 and died in 1956. It was surprisingly easy with their new computers. By now, I almost expected the information that the assistant gave me: that János had been born on 23 October.

That was my birthday, too.

I was now sure that all these facts about his life and mine were not just the same by chance. I believed my doppelgänger was trying to tell me something important, but I didn't know what. I wanted to talk about it with Andrea, but that still seemed impossible. First of all, she wouldn't listen to me, and then even if she did listen I didn't think she would understand. Or she wouldn't want to understand because she was too worried by the story. I decided to wait and see if I could meet my doppelgänger again on 18 January.

Chapter 16 *It all happens again*

Every night from then on I had the dream in all its possible forms – the opening door, the running man, the loud noise, the man who was looking for something. Sometimes it was me who ran out of the door, and sometimes it was me who was knocked onto the ground; sometimes I was looking for something, sometimes I was watching the man looking for something. And behind everything I could hear a man's voice shouting, 'Help me!' and 'Andrea, Kati!'

Again and again I woke up hot, cold, crying, shouting and always terribly afraid. I didn't tell Andrea, but I knew she knew. I could tell she had woken up when I did, although she never said anything. I felt that she, too, was afraid of what was happening to me.

*   *   *

Saturday 18 January was a grey, cold winter's day. It wasn't snowing, but it looked as if it would soon. I got up early and went to work. My boss had asked me to go into the office and go through a new work plan with him, before talking about it with the other people on Monday. It took much longer than expected and I didn't get home until half past six.

'Hello!' I shouted as I walked through the door of our flat. 'Hello. Where are you?'

There was no reply. I walked into the living room and there on the table was a note.

Dear John,
Zsolt phoned. His mother's ill and I offered to
look after the bar while he takes her to the doctor's.
I couldn't get Petra to look after Kati, so I've taken
her with me. Won't be long I hope!
See you later.
Love,
Andrea (and Kati) xxx

My blood went cold. I looked at my watch. It was quarter to seven. I ran into the hall, forgetting my coat, and ran downstairs and out into the street. Then I started running towards the bar. It was nearly five to seven. I turned right into Felka utca – not left into Gergely utca – and ran up to number 7. The big front door was open. I went inside, I was breathing quickly because I'd been running. I could hear the noise of a television or radio from one of the flats.

Suddenly, there was a very loud noise like a bomb from outside somewhere. All the windows shook. One or two windows opened, and voices called out to each other in the dark.

'What was that?' asked one.

'I don't know,' someone replied.

'It sounded like an bomb,' said a third.

Just then, I heard someone shouting outside in the street. 'Help! Help! There's been an explosion in Gergely utca. Help everybody!'

I ran out of the building, the door shutting loudly behind me.

In the street, I ran straight into someone.

'Look out!' said a man.

He fell to the ground. I looked down, asking myself what I was going to see. There the man who looked like me lying on the ground.

'Sorry . . . ' I said in Hungarian.

And then I ran along Felka utca and crossed over the road. My mind was racing. I was thinking all the time about what I was going to find.

Chapter 17 *We must get them out!*

When I turned into Gergely utca I stopped running. It was difficult to see where I was going. The street was full of smoke, like a thick grey cloud everywhere. I couldn't see anything, and the smell of gas was terrible. Perhaps a gas pipe in one of the old buildings had broken, and that had started the explosion.

I took my handkerchief out and put it across my mouth and nose, and walked along the street. There was also the loud noise of car alarms ringing – started by the explosion. I found I was walking on glass from all the broken windows. People were already trying to knock out the other pieces of glass from their windows, and some had started to put paper and plastic over them to keep their flats warm.

I knew I had got to Zsolt's bar because there was a small crowd of people standing around it. I looked down; there was nothing left. I couldn't see the steps going down, the windows or even the walls – there was just a lot of broken stones. I looked and looked, my mind completely empty.

Suddenly, I understood what had happened.

'My wife!' I shouted in Hungarian. 'My wife and daughter are in there. We must get them out! Help me!'

People looked at me.

'Come on,' I said, looking at the people standing around. 'We must get them out!'

I started to give orders. I made everybody stand in a line, and told them to pass along the stones from the destroyed building and put them in the street. Then I got to work, picking up the broken pieces of wood and stone. The people soon got the idea, and we worked as a good team. I was very pleased to see other neighbours coming and joining in on the other side of what had been the front of the bar. Surprisingly soon, I was down to where the doorway had been.

At that moment, I heard the noise of police cars, fire engines and ambulances coming closer, and the people I was working with stopped helping me.

'What's the matter?' I shouted. 'We must get my wife and . . . '

'Come on out, sir, please,' said a voice. I looked up. In the grey light the person who had spoken looked very big and black above me.

'But my wife and my daughter are in here,' I shouted. 'We must get them out!'

And I threw the pieces of wood and stone that I had in my hands up into the street, and turned to get some more from the destroyed doorway. But then strong hands got hold of me and pulled me up into the street.

'Just come out of the way, sir,' said the voice.

'But my wife . . . !'

'I understand, sir,' said the voice, which I now realised came from a fireman, 'but it's too dangerous for you to go in there. Leave it to us. The place is full of gas – can't you smell it?'

I could smell it now I had stopped. And I could feel it inside my body.

The fireman let me go, and I fell down onto the street and started crying.

I was lifted up by more hands, and soon I was lying in the back of an ambulance parked a few metres down the street. I was coughing a lot, so a nurse put something over my face to help me breathe. I started to feel better and tried to sit up.

'Just lie down, please,' said the nurse. 'You need to rest for a while.'

'But my wife and daughter were in that cellar,' I said. 'I have to find them.'

'There's nothing you can do now, sir,' said the voice in a very gentle way. 'Just rest.'

I must have slept for a few minutes. When I woke, I sat up. Then I stood up and stepped out into the street. The ambulance men were standing outside.

'Are you feeling any better, sir?' one of them asked.

'Yes, much better, thanks,' I replied. 'Is there any news?'

'Not yet, sir,' said another ambulance man.

I pushed my way through the crowd, which was much bigger now. The air was clearer, too, but the street was full of blue lights. The firemen had put some lights in front of Zsolt's bar so that they could see what they were doing, and the police were keeping people away.

I called to one of the policemen and explained that I was the husband of someone who had been in the cellar, and he took me over to a police van on the other side of the street.

'Good evening, sir,' said a young policeman sitting inside the van. 'Take a seat.'

I sat down opposite him.

'Is there any news yet?' I asked him.

'Not yet, I'm afraid, sir,' he said, looking serious. 'Could I ask you for some information, please?'

And for the next five minutes I gave him facts and dates about myself, Andrea and Kati, which he wrote down on many different pieces of paper. He also asked me what I knew about the bar and the people who worked there, and who might have been inside when the explosion happened.

'What shall I do now?' I asked, feeling very unsure of myself.

'Well, sir,' he replied, 'you live nearby, so why don't you go home and wait there? I've got your telephone number and I'll call you as soon as we have any news.'

'OK,' I said. 'Thanks.'

I got out of the van, and pushed back through the crowd, leaving the lights and the noise behind me. I felt terrible. Deep inside I didn't believe that anybody in that cellar could have lived through the explosion. The bar was completely destroyed. It was impossible for Andrea and Kati to be alive.

I then started thinking about how stupid I'd been. Why hadn't I told Andrea what I'd seen in my dreams and what I'd found out from Mrs Fischer? I couldn't believe I had killed my own wife and child. And all because I was too interested in the doppelgänger story to think carefully about the two people I loved most in the world. Too interested in the doppelgänger story to think about what my doppelgänger wanted to tell me . . . How stupid I'd been! The bar had been destroyed. My wife and child had been destroyed. And my life was now destroyed. I would never be happy again.

Chapter 18   *Unexpected help*

I was walking along Gergely utca very slowly, feeling as if I wanted to die. I wasn't looking where I was going. I was looking down at the ground, lost in my thoughts. Suddenly, when I got to the corner of the street, I walked into somebody.

'Sorry,' I said, looking up.

I saw it was someone like me I was looking at. It was my doppelgänger again. We looked into each other's eyes. And then he lifted his arm and pointed his finger. I looked where he was pointing, and I could see two small people at the end of the dark street. One was a woman and one was a child. I couldn't believe my eyes.

'Andrea!' I shouted. 'Kati!'

As I started to run towards them, I looked back at the man.

There was no-one there.

We all three ran to each other, and held each other for a long time.

'Thank goodness!' I said at last. 'I thought . . . I thought you were . . . '

'Sssh,' said Andrea, putting her hand over my mouth. 'And we would be, but for your "friend".'

'What friend?' I asked. 'Zsolt?'

'No, John,' she said, laughing. 'Your doppelgänger.'

'My . . . ?' I stood with my mouth open. 'What on earth do you mean?'

And so Andrea explained to me what had happened.

'I walked round to the bar with Kati, ready to help while Zsolt was away at the doctor's. Zsolt was already standing in the street when I got there. He told me there was no-one in the bar, and so we stood talking in the street for a few minutes. Then he got into his car and went off to take his mother to the doctor's. When I turned round to go down to the bar, I saw you standing in front of the entrance. I called your name, and asked you what you wanted. But you said nothing, and I tried to go down into the bar. You didn't move. I asked you to get out of the way, but you didn't. And then Kati started crying. I asked her what the matter was. "See what you've done now, John – you've made her cry." I said to you. Kati was crying and shaking her head. "Not Daddy," she said. "Not Daddy."

I looked at the man in front of me again, as carefully as I could in the dark winter light . . . and then I realised it must be your doppelgänger. The coat was different – it looked old-fashioned. Suddenly, I remembered what it had said about doppelgängers in that book you'd brought home: "*it can sometimes be seen by somebody close if it has an important message*". As I looked, the man pointed down the street. I looked where he was pointing. There was nothing.

I looked at the man and asked him what he meant. Again the man pointed down the street, and finally I understood that he wanted me to go away. So I did. I walked home. When we got home, Kati fell asleep on the sofa. While she was sleeping I made some tea. Suddenly, I heard a loud noise like a bomb from somewhere outside. It sounded quite far away. It took me some time to wake Kati and get her dressed again, and we came to see what had happened. Of course, I was really afraid that you had been in the bar, John.'

We looked at each other as we reached the outside door of the block of flats where we lived.

'This is a very strange story,' I said.

'It certainly is,' said Andrea. 'You must write it down.'

'I will,' I said.

And we went inside and shut out the night.

A note on the pronunciation of the Hungarian words in the story

Felka: /felkɑ/
Utca: /uːtsɑ/
Gergely: /gergei/
Váci: /vɑːtsiː/
János: /jɑːnoʃ/
Szabó: /sɑboː/
Zsolt: /ʒolt/
Kati: /kɑtiː/